The Complete Guide
to Michigan Fossils

Joseph J. "PaleoJoe" Kchodl

The Complete Guide to Michigan Fossils

by
Joseph J. Kchodl

Photos by Joseph J. Kchodl
and
Rodger Chase,
Photographic Reverie

The University of Michigan Press
Ann Arbor

&

Petoskey Publishing Company
Traverse City

Dedication

To my mom and dad,
who instilled in me the love of all things natural
and the desire to learn more

Copyright © 2006 by Joseph J. Kchodl
All rights reserved

Published in the United States of America by
The University of Michigan Press
&
The Petoskey Publishing Company
Manufactured in the United States of America
2007   2006   4   3   2   1
ISBN-10: 472-03149-X
ISBN-13: 978-0-472-03149-8
Library of Congress Cataloging-in-Publication Data on File

Contents

Site Map

Fossil invertebrate sites as well as fossil mammal sites are too numerous to show on this map. Michigan is very fossil rich and depending on the types of fossils sought, varied in locations.

This map gives only a general overview of fossil locations throughout the state.

Introduction

"...in disclosing the past of the earth...the mind of man is cultivated and kept open...."
- Leonardo DaVinci

Discovery – what make fossils so fun to find? As a youth in a fossil rich part of the United States, I would spend countless hours wandering through the woods and fields looking for anything unusual. I loved to wander through nature observing everything I could. Often I would kick over a rock or stone and see something quite unusual. That "thing," I would later find out, was a fossil. In some cases I would find a sea shell imprint, a sea shell so far away from any water? I had no idea of the joy and wonderment to come.

I soon bought my first book about fossils, a simple fieldguide to the creatures from the ancient Paleozic. It contained pictures and descriptions of creatures long since extinct. It had dinosaurs, sea shells, trilobites, crinoids, corals and the list goes on. The one major problem for me was that the monsters we call dinosaurs never lived near where I lived. I was only 10 years old and my father was not about to give me the car keys to drive out to the badlands and find dinosaurs. But the joy of discovery was great nonetheless. For a youth this discovery was special. It allowed for deep thought, imagination and dreams of times long ago.

Much of the ground was under water millions of years ago, much like the State of Michigan. In fact most of the fossils I found as a child were the same as can be found in Alpena, Charlevoix, Traverse City and many other areas of the state.

The Upper Penninsula of Michigan is rich as well, but not with fossils. The U.P. has vast deposits of igneous rocks including copper and iron ore. There are few fossils found there, but only along the southern shore line pushed up by the wave and ice activity of Lake Michigan. These fossils are washed up from the depths of the lake which does contain fossil bearing layers.

Discovery – what has been discovered? Many of the fossil finds of scientific importance have been made by amateurs. There are not enough paleontologists around to find all important sites and fossils. It is up to many amateurs to find and describe the fossils.

As development encroaches, many fossil sites are in danger of being lost forever. Many rich sites have already been lost. Amateur or professional, take the time to visit local and statewide sites often. It is a wonderful way to spend time outdoors with your family discovering new things together, taking part in a fun activity. Who knows, you may discover something new and exciting.

Types of Rocks

There are several types of rock found in Michigan.

Igneous rock from the Upper Peninsula: Bonus
matrix rock, copper and prenite, Kewenaw Peninsula

Igneous rock

This rock is formed by volcanic activity. This type of rock is formed in the super-heated core of the earth. Igneous rock is formed by molten magma. Volcanos and the super-heated magma that rises to the surface would burn away all remains of anything organic. There are no fossils found in igneous rock.

Metamorphic rock

This rock is comprised ostensibly of sedimentary rock. It has been deformed by heat and pressure below the earth's surface. This type of rock is generally rock that has been heated and/or twisted by the earth. Sometimes remains can be found in this type of rock, but often it is distorted by the pressure of earth around it.

Sedimentary rock

This rock is usually made up of weathered or eroded igneous rock in the form of sand and dirt. Sedimentary rock is formed by successive layers of sediment – rock, dirt and sand – being deposited one on top of another. This is the type of rock that contains the most fossil evidence. An organism, plant or animal falls to the ground and is buried by layers of earth. But in order to create a fossil certain circumstances must be in place. Finding a fossil, though

**Sedimentary rock showing various layers of sediment,
best type of rock to look in**

sometimes common, belies the fact that most organisms
never fossilize. What you may find in your lifetime is but a
very small fraction of what was alive on earth.

Fossils are normally found in sedimentary rock
deposits. Michigan has many areas where sedimentary
rock deposits are exposed. These are the most favorable
for finding fossils.

Time

Many people measure the passage of time in years or
decades. A long time ago could be measured in hundreds
if not thousands of years. Remember the pyramids were

built over 5200 thousand years ago. But when we think of geological time and the process of fossilization, we speak in terms of tens of thousands, hundreds of thousands and even millions of years. Burial of an organism happens quite rapidly, but subsequent deposition, sedimentation and fossilization takes millions of years. Finally, tectonic upheaval, weathering and erosion that may take millions of years, eventually exposes the fossil.Then it is discovered and prepared.

Geological Time Chart

This chart of geological time will give you an idea of the enormous amount of time that has passed in the earth's history. There has been ample time for evolution and the diversification of life on earth.

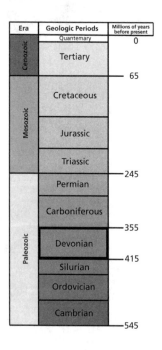

Era	Geologic Periods	Millions of years before present
Cenozoic	Quantemary	0
Cenozoic	Tertiary	
Cenozoic		65
Mesozoic	Cretaceous	
Mesozoic	Jurassic	
Mesozoic	Triassic	
Mesozoic		245
Paleozoic	Permian	
Paleozoic	Carboniferous	
Paleozoic		355
Paleozoic	Devonian	
Paleozoic		415
Paleozoic	Silurian	
Paleozoic	Ordovician	
Paleozoic	Cambrian	
Paleozoic		545

What Is a Fossil?

A very short and simple definition of fossils is as follows:

Fossils are the remains of something that was alive a very long time ago, have since died and turned to stone.

Further, the organism must have hard parts like shell or bone because the soft tissues usually decay away prior to fossilization.

Yes, it is a very simple definition, but that is want a fossil is. Although we can find lots of fossils, there are special circumstances that need to be in place before an organism can become a fossil. Of the uncountable billions and billions of organisms that once lived; only a small portion of what was once alive can be found as fossils.

In order to become a fossil, it has to have been alive; an organic plant or animal. It has to have had hard parts and it has to have been buried very quickly to prevent decay. Fossils are the remains, the evidence of these plants and animals. These remains can take many forms.

There are many ways the fossil can be preserved. Eight of the most prevalent ways fossils are preserved are:

Mineralization or replacement
Preservation in tar and amber
Molds and casts
Drying or desiccation
Carbonization
Freezing (Ice Age)
Castings and coprolites
Simple burial

There are two major types of fossils. The actual fossil that is formed by means identified above, such as bones, plants, or sea shells, and secondly, *trace fossils,* such as trails, tracks, burrows and imprints.

A *trace fossil* gives us evidence that something was there, passed by or existed. The most commonly known trace fossils are dinosaur footprints. There are many more trace fossils than just tracks.

Worm borings
in sandstone,
Devonian Period

Nature will not be denied. Nature is the same today as it was millions of years ago and will be in the future. There are certain natural laws and ways that creatures behave that will not change. There are creatures such as mollusks and worms that crawl through the sea floor, terrestrial dirt and sediments. As these creatures crawl through the sediments, they leave trails. In some cases the sea creatures secrete a substance to harden the burrow guarding against collapsing. These burrows then fill with softer sediment. The sediment will begin to harden over time, forming rock. Millions of years later underlying rock can weather to the surface, and the softer sediments in the burrows will weather away leaving the burrowed holes behind, thus giving us evidence that something had been here. The actual creature, mollusk or worm was long since gone and in many cases we do not even know the species of creature that made the burrow, but it proves the evidence of some creature's existence, so many millions of years ago.

Dinosaur and other tracks are also formed, showing us the presence of ancient creatures. In this case the tracks or footprints are left in a soft muddy plain or swamp. As the mud hardens, other sediments cover the tracks and over millions of years, the area fossilizes. After a while weathering begins exposing the tracks of those creatures that lived so long ago. Tracks are also trace fossils. The original creature has long since passed by, but we have evidence of something that passed by.

How Are Fossils Formed?

Most fossils are formed by a process called permineralization or mineral replacement. There are two very important components in the formation of these fossils.

1. These remains must be covered rapidly in dirt that contains chemicals and minerals. If the fossil is not covered quickly, the organism will decay rapidly and scavengers can widely scatter the remains.

2. There must be lots of water continuously or periodically in large amounts. The water also contains lots of chemicals and minerals.

Replacement and permineralization

First the organism must be covered by dirt, sand, mud or some other such sediment. This is quite critical as all living organisms are prone to decay. Atmospheric elements, such as rain coupled with bacterial decay, and action by scavengers, affects the amount of fossilization of any organism. Rain and the action of water as in floods can deteriorate the organism. Water also aids in decay of the creatures. As animals decay the action of moving water also can disarticulate (break apart) the remains. Rapid covering by sediment prevents disturbing the remains by water and scavengers from eating or tearing apart the carcass. Exposure to the elements is the worst thing that can happen to a potential fossil. Fossils formed by replacement can be found in Michigan.

Secondly, in the formation of permineralized and replacement fossils, the availability of water after the organism is buried is quite critical.

Permineralization occurs when open spaces in the organism are replaced by minerals, such as calcite, dolomite, silica and other substances that are contained as dissolved components in the water. As a creature decays or dissolves, it is replaced by these chemicals and minerals. Sometimes this is also called petrification. Replacement is similar and occurs when the organism decays completely and is replaced by minerals. Permineralized fossils can also be found in Michigan.

Preservation in tar and amber

Usually this type of preservation is quite rare and only found in several locations on earth. The LaBrea Tar Pits in California and a similar tar pit in Poland do yield numerous fossils that have been preserved in the tar. The soft sticky substance traps animals and plant material. The organisms sink into the tar, soft tissues dissolve and the hard parts are left behind. This type of fossil is not found in Michigan.

Insect trapped in tar,
LaBrea Tar Pits, LaBrea, California

Amber is formed by the hardening or fossilization of conifer tree sap. Again nature shows us today what could have happened a long time ago. Today, if a branch is broken off a pine tree, the tree will start to exude sap just like it did thousands of years ago. Back then, perhaps broken by a strong wind or maybe a Mastodon walking by, the tree exuded sap. Then insects drawn to the sweet sticky smell or just unfortunate to cross the sticky sap got stuck. After the sap dried, it fell to the forest floor beginning its long process of fossilization. This type of fossil has not been found in Michigan.

Midge in amber,
Baltic region, Russia

Molds and casts

Sometimes the organism completely decays in the sediments before any mineralization occurs, leaving a cavity in the sediment. The cavity is subsequently filled with other material such as dolomite, calcite, pyrite or some other material, leaving a cast of the original organism. These types of fossils are also quite common. The cast is often an exact replica of the organism. This type of fossil can be found in Michigan.

Drying or desiccation

This type of fossilization is very rare. There have only been less than a dozen dried specimens found. Humans have been creating mummies for nearly 5000 years, but nature has done this on rare occasions for about 10,000 years. In Australia one such fossil was recovered from a cave. It was the fossilized remains of a giant moa, a large bird species now extinct. The creature perished and somehow the leg bone, complete with desiccated skin, muscle tissues, tendons, feathers and claws, was discovered. This type of fossil is not found in Michigan.

Carbonization

This form of fossilization usually reserved for plant matter and material. It is also called carbon film. The plant tissues, such as leaves, usually decay; organic elements dissolve away, leaving carbon which leaves a dark film in the rock that shows the veins and outline of the leaf. Often when there is sufficient tissue available, such as branches and twigs, the fossil remains resemble coal. If enough of this material is available, it does turn into coal and other fossil fuels like oil. This type of fossil could be found in Michigan. Fossil fuels, such as oil, have and continue to be found in Michigan.

Freezing

This is another rare form of fossilization. Mostly creatures from the last Ice Age are preserved in this manner. As one might imagine, frozen fossils are found in Siberia, Alaska, Russia and Canada. For several decades paleontologists have been finding the fossilized remains of Mammoths in Siberia and Alaska. The creatures are remarkably preserved. Skin, hair, muscle tissues, internal organs are all beautifully preserved. Scientists have even combed the Mammoth hair and found plant and tree spores and pollen, giving us evidence of the type of plants and trees that were alive when that Mammoth died. This type of fossil cannot be found in Michigan.

Castings and coprolites

This type of fossil is also a trace fossil. Coprolites and castings are the remains of fossilized excrement. Again, they are a trace and usually cannot be identified as to what type of creature left them. These coprolites are also very interesting to paleontologists as they sometimes contain remains of seeds and plants for herbivores and even bone fragments and other items for carnivores, indicating what the creature's diet consisted of. This type of fossil is not found in Michigan.

Unknown coprolite, Green River Formation, Wyoming

How and Where to Find Fossils

Once you learn what to look for and where, fossils are quite easy to find. Usually paleontologists let Mother Nature help by weathering rock outcroppings. You can find these areas by going to cliffs, lakeshores and other locations where rock has been exposed naturally. Other locations are discovered with the help of man. Road cuts, railroad cuts, major excavations as well as quarries are excellent areas in which to look for fossils.

Limestone by its very nature is a wonderful rock to look in. Limestone is created from the remains of ancient reef building creatures like corals, crinoids and sea shells. This type of stone is very hard and therefore sought after as a building material as well as bedding for railroads and driveways. Limestone, however, is a very hard rock to clean and prepare fossils in. Some of the best fossilization of organisms is found in limestone, but very specific tools are required to free them from the limestone matrix. Shale is much softer and breaks easily exposing the fossils within. Little cleaning is needed with shale so as a beginner, look for shale outcroppings.

There is no substitute for knowing the geological formations of the area you will be searching in.

You can start looking for fossils by doing a little bit of research. Seek out local fossil collectors; join a local fossil or rock and mineral club. There is no reason to explore the entire state on your own when there is a wealth of knowledge available for you to narrow the search areas. Fossil collectors often are very helpful to beginners by telling them some of the best areas to collect in. Local libraries can provide general information about areas where fossils are found. University libraries also have a wealth of knowledge specific to geological and paleontological sites. Today, with the availability of the internet, you can also find many fossil sites as well as directions to them. Some of the best publications to look through are the field trip guidebooks found in university libraries.

The University of Michigan has a tremendous amount of fossil specific pamphlets that are available for purchase. A complete listing of publications and price list is available from:

Publications
Museum of Paleontology
The University of Michigan
1529 Ruthven Museums Building
1109 Geddes Road
Ann Arbor, Michigan
PaleoPubs@umich.edu

These not only describe the fossils, but also often describe where they can be found.

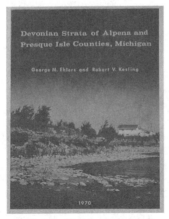

Example of a field trip guidebook

Maps, such as the USGS (United States Geological Service) topographical maps as well as the Michigan Gazetteer, also are very helpful. Once you hear of, or have researched a location, these maps will direct you to the locations described. Specifically these maps do show quarries which sometimes can be loaded with fossils. The topographical maps are also quite valuable to locate specific elevations, cliffs and embankments. Topographical maps of your areas can generally be found or ordered in outdoor retail stores, local DNR or county conservation district offices. They can also be ordered over the internet.

Photo of USGS topographical map

Fossils in Michigan

Fossils can be found in many parts of Michigan. The state was once the bottom of a shallow salt water tropical sea. After millions of years of deposition and sedimentation, the fossils were buried deep within the earth. Thanks to plate tectonics and a series of ice age events, times when glaciers cut across Michigan, overlying layers of earth were scraped away, once again exposing the ancient sea floor now turned into fossils.

One of the neatest and most common type of fossil is really not just one fossil. There is a type of fossil some paleontologists call "hash." Basically, "hash" is all the organic matter that settles to the bottom of the ocean prior to the seabed being covered by sediments. Once the bed is covered, it then becomes fossilized. The "hash" normally contains the remnants of plants and animals that have died and fallen to the seafloor. Crinoids, corals, echinoderms, and brachiopods normally make up this "hash." Occasionally trilobite pieces, such as head sections or tail sections and even segments, can be found. When you find and look at this "hash" solidified as a rock, what you are seeing is a piece of the ancient seafloor as it was millions of years ago. The "hash" in the photo below is on a rock in the breakwater in Petoskey.

Example of "hash" containing fossils

Michigan during the Paleozoic Era

The Paleozoic period means the period of time when life began to emerge through to the first major extinction around 250 million years ago. The Paleozoic period covers the Cambrian through Permian periods spanning some 345 million years.

During much of the Paleozoic period there were many coral reefs that formed and provided sanctuary for a wide variety of sea life much as modern coral reefs provide habitats for today's sea creatures. The sea level would rise and fall over time – literally over millions of years. Many different creatures lived and thrived here. The rich coral reefs that were formed over time actually form the bedrock in parts of the state, most notably in the northern Lower Peninsula. As an example of the rich flora and fauna that lived long ago, one may find many of the over 200 species of prehistoric life that inhabited the area around Alpena. Corals, crinoids, bryozoans, gastropods, brachiopods, cephalopods, trilobites and very primitive fish and sharks swam and lived here. All of these fossils may be found here.

Michigan during the Pleistocene Epoch

The Pleistocene Epoch was from about 1.8 million years ago to about 11,000 million years ago. During the Pleistocene, large global glaciers advanced and retreated 4 times across Michigan. Before, during and after the period of the last Ice Age, Michigan was very similar to the Michigan we know now. The state was covered in cedar and fir tree forests. Many species of deciduous trees also were present. The elevation changes of the current terrain were caused by glaciers as they flowed and retreated. Beach sand can be found many miles inland, and in some areas of the state, the sand can be dozens if not hundreds of feet thick. Swamps were also quite common in lower areas. The temperature was a bit warmer than we now know between the periods of glaciation.

Over hundreds of years as the glaciers retreated, animals started to follow the glaciers retreat back to the north. Animals, such as giant beaver, giant deer, large bison, mammoths and mastodons, could be found across the state.

During the period between about 10,000 years ago and 5,000 years ago many of the large mammals died out. Some paleontologists believe it was in part due to human predation and the change in climate. In fact, some of the Mastodon bones found across the state show evidence of butchering marks left behind by ancient man and his stone knives.

What kind of fossils can we find here?

Across most of the northern part of the State of Michigan, what I call the fossil crescent from Alpena through Rogers City, Cheboygan, Petoskey, Charlevoix through to Traverse City and a bit further south, fossils from the Paleozoic are quite common.

Most fossils are found nearer to the shores of the Great Lakes because of the erosion that takes place on the shore. Here the bedrock and land meet the water, and layers containing fossils are exposed by wave and water action. The further you move inland, the fewer fossils are found due to the build up of layers of dirt covering the fossil-laden sediments. Also the glacial till covering the land is much thicker, and the fossil-bearing sediments are therefore buried deeper. However, quarries inland do expose the fossil-bearing sediments and fossils can be found at such quarries.

The fossils found here are marine, which means, they were animals and plants that lived in salt water seas. Michigan was once the bottom of a shallow salt water tropical sea. We know this because of the flora and fauna we find. The area of the northern Lower Peninsula abounds with corals. Corals normally grow in shallow salt water tropical seas. Today the area of Michigan tends to get very cold, not a great deal of warm water. We do have a great deal of fresh water, not salt water. So how and why do we find fossils of salt water marine creatures here in Michigan?

Plate tectonics is the answer. The earth is dynamic and constantly moving and shifting. Volcanos erupt, earthquakes shake the earth, mountains are being pushed up and great valleys are being created. Michigan is located on a tectonic plate called the North American plate. The plate is roughly the size of North America. It is moving almost imperceptibly to the northwest all the time. We cannot feel it, but that doesn't mean it isn't happening. The North American plate is hitting the Pacific plate out near California. The Pacific plate runs from California up towards Alaska, over to Japan, down near Indonesia towards Australia, past Antarctica and along the western coast of South America all the way back to California. The plate is so large that as the North

American plate hits the Pacific plate, the Pacific plate doesn't move. The North American plate pushes against the Pacific plate until enough pressure exists to cause an earthquake. Buildings rock and fall, sometimes people get hurt but the North American plate pushes under the Pacific plate by a little bit, moving North America to the northwest.

350 million years ago, Michigan was located near the equator. Now here we are in Michigan. Who knows, in another 350 million years we could be somewhere near Alaska, who knows? That is why Michigan was once a shallow salt water tropical sea. Hence the type of fossils we find here most are those of creatures that lived in the sea.

Fossil site off Burkholder Road in Alpena, Michigan

Before You Go Collecting

The following information is provided so you can enjoy a great outdoor activity. Laws governing public lands, state forests and national parks must be followed. Fines can add up to quite a large sum for disobeying the laws. Also if fossil outcroppings are located on private land, it is highly recommended that permission be obtained prior to gaining access to the property. Whether fossil hunting with the family or by yourself, some prior planning is necessary for a rewarding excursion. Familiarize yourself with the following sections, and as you gain in experience, you can add, delete or substitute for your own needs. Whether on public or private land, a good rule of thumb is pack out whatever you pack in.

Safety, courtesy and dig etiquette

First of all, honor and respect the outdoors. Nature is here for us to enjoy and preserve for future generations. Respect for nature begins with keeping nature clean.

Pack out your trash. Don't leave pop cans, paper bags or any other trash on public or private land. Not only is it against the law to litter, but also if you are on private land and litter, the landowner may not allow you or anyone else access to the property.

Secondly, take only what you need and work only in an area you can easily work. When digging, disrupt the site as minimally as possible. Don't dig so many holes that the area looks like the moon. When you are done digging in a fossil area, it is not necessary to cover your dig site. Leaving the area excavated will help the paleontologist who follows you.

It is important to dig slowly, dig deliberately and examine every piece of rock that breaks away. In many cases as the rock breaks or cleaves, pieces of the fossil remain in the counterpart (the piece that breaks away). Keep these broken counterparts, pack them up and bring them home too. Valuable pieces from the counterparts can be retrieved during preparation.

Tools and equipment

This is a list of items you may want to bring with you to the field. It is by no means the final list of items you will need. Some of these items are common sense items and are self-explanatory. Others are comfort items that will help you enjoy your collecting trip. If you are walking a long way to the dig site, use common sense and carry only what you need. The trip will get very tiring if you are bringing along the kitchen sink. This is only a guide to help you decide what you may need.

Backpack
Safety glasses
2 inch paintbrush
Sun tan lotion
Magnifying glass
Dental picks
Duct tape
Compass
Pencil
Walking stick
Gloves
Shovel
1/2 inch brush
Handy wipes

Pry bar
Heavy blanket
Bottled water
Camera
Diluted white
  glue
Insect repellant
Geological
  hammer
Chisels (various
  sizes)
Hard hat (when
  in quarries)
Empty film con-
  tainers

Cardboard pop
  or beer shells
Knee pads
  or padding
Topographical
  maps
Notebook or
  3"x 5"cards
Sharpie or
  marking pen
Good steel-toed
  shoes or hik-
  ing boots

Take snack foods and drinking water along with you as well. From personal experience, you may stay out in the woods for quite a while. Carry newspaper, toilet paper or cotton batting in order to wrap some of the delicate fossils you find. Also the empty film containers can hold some of the smaller and more delicate fossils.

Collecting Fossils

Removing fossils from the rock

Sometimes it may be more acceptable to leave the fossil as you find it. Leaving it in the rock sometimes makes the fossil look more dramatic. But sometimes removing the fossil from the rock is what you'll want to do. It is all a matter of personal choice.

The tools and techniques needed to remove fossils really depend on the type of rock the fossil material is in. Shale and limestone are the most common rocks that fossils are found in and both types require widely varied techniques for removal. The rock material, whether shale or limestone, is generally called matrix. Shale can usually be identified by looking at the side or profile of the rock. It usually has lines of sedimentation, different colors of rock that look like they have been stacked one upon the other. These are also called bedding planes. The color of shale is usually light to dark grey and almost to black. Shale also being very brittle has cracks that are parallel to the surface of the rock. Limestone is usually very uniform. It is usually impossible to find bedding layers. Striking a piece of limestone with a hammer can result in the rock breaking in many directions. Limestone is also a very hard rock, but usually fossils are very well preserved in this type of matrix. The color of limestone varies but is usually cream to tan in color.

Shale by far is the easiest matrix to remove fossils from. This sedimentary rock is usually quite brittle. A simple chisel and hammer will allow you to expose the fossils in the matrix. By placing a chisel along one of the cracks, colored lines or bedding planes, and striking it with a hammer, you can break the rock parallel to the surface. I liken it to opening a book. If fossils are there, it is like reading the pages of a prehistoric book. If there are fossils present, cleaning them can also be fairly easy. By using dental picks and pin vises, bits of matrix can be picked or removed from the area on and surrounding the fossil. Shale has a high moisture content and can begin to deteriorate rapidly. As the fossil and shale dries, the fossil itself can begin to crack and break apart. Have some Crazy Glue ™ on hand and some diluted white glue to apply to the fossil in order to "set" it and prevent further decay and breakage.

Limestone is a totally different type of matrix. This rock is very hard and does not break easily. In many cases it breaks in many different directions sometimes revealing a small piece of a fossil. In many cases it will reveal only a profile of the fossil. It is sometimes necessary to study and research in order to be able to identify the fact that fossils are present. Using a hammer and chisel is the way to break the matrix into smaller pieces. Dental picks and pin vises can still be used to remove bits of matrix from the fossil, but it is very time consuming. There are several very specialized tools that will help in matrix removal.

Professional tools

Some of the professional and expensive tools can be replaced by some more inexpensive and readily available tools. The major differences between the professional tools and the others are that the professional tools are larger, faster and more expensive.

The professional tools consist of an air compressor, a prep box, a stereomicroscope and several air tools such as an air chisel and an air abrasive unit. The air abrasive unit is just a mini sandblaster.

First a prep box is recommended. Due to the flying dust and debris and powders used with the air abrasive unit, a prep box is essential and will contain all the above. The box can be constructed out of wood, with two arm holes in the sides and a glass viewing port in the top. The stereomicroscope is mounted to the top so viewing through the glass window is possible. Also there needs to be an evacuation fan to pull the dust away from the area you will be working.

When working with limestone, the air chisel can help remove, break away the matrix. The air abrasive unit is used with several different types of powder and medium that will act as a sandblaster and literally blast away the matrix from the fossil. This will take a great deal of patience, trial and error and more than a few damaged fossils to perfect.

Some simple tools that are available on the market that will not require so much time, energy and effort to set up. First of all, a simple engraving tool will take the place of an air chisel. The tool will not be as swift or effective. You will need to spend more time breaking away the matrix, but the result will be the same. Break the matrix away as close to the fossil as you can without actually hitting the fossil. Then a simple pin vise or dental pick can then be used to finish the job, picking away the last bits of matrix; however, it will be time consuming. If a sand blaster is preferred, there is one item on the market that is a much smaller and cheaper alternative. It is made by Passche. This company is well known for the model air paint sprayers it manufactures. It also makes an air abrasive unit. It is generally less that $100 and again is smaller and it takes more time to get the same results. For this option you must make a prep box to contain the powders. These powders are very dangerous to the respiratory system and are a breathing hazard.

It will take much practice coupled with trial and error and of course patience in order to get better in removing the matrix from the fossils you find.

The best place to find fossils

Before we start describing where to look, I have to tell you a few surprising secrets. I have traveled around the state looking for fossils, speaking to kids in schools and just driving from one location to another and made a startling discovery. Limestone is a commercially quarried rock valuable for its hardness and beauty. Sometimes it can turn up in the funniest places. You also have to remember that limestone and the bedrock of Michigan is millions of years old. During the passage of time Michigan was covered in water several times. There were several glaciers and the associated rivers and water action acted upon the rocks. There are several locations in the state where for lack of a better word, river rock, can be found and quarried. This rock and weathered limestone is used by landscaping contractors, construction companies and homeowners. I have found fossils in the outdoor landscaping stone of fast food restaurants. I have found fossils in my friends crushed stone driveways and along railroad tracks used as bedding for the railroad ties. Sometimes you can find fossils in the strangest places, keep your eyes open.

Fossils are found in sedimentary rock. The best places to look for fossils in the State of Michigan are in the northern Lower Peninsula. Areas near the Lake Huron and Lake Michigan rocky shorelines are found especially to be fossiliferous. Sedimentary rock in this area is fairly close to the

Example of rock outcroppings at the edges
of Michigan roadways

surface, especially near roadcuts and the lakeshore. Limestone quarries also dot most of the counties in the Lower Peninsula. Quarries are also fossil hot spots.

Roadcut Route 23 north of Presque Isle

Example of hexagonaria coral from this site

Roadcuts – Look near the base of roadcuts, but please be careful and watch out for traffic. Place the car in such a way as not to obstruct traffic. Bring along a hammer and chisel as well as some good boots or shoes. As you inspect the rocks look vertically through one layer at a time in one area in front of you. When you find a layer that seems to contain fossils, then follow that layer horizontally to maximize your effort and find more fossils. When digging on the walls of the roadcut, be aware that loosening lower rocks could cause rocks higher up to fall. **Be careful.**

Lakeshores – Looking near the lakeshores can be fun but also you need to be careful. Sandy shorelines will probably not yield fossils. Go to lakeshores with rocky outcroppings. Again be careful as you remove lower rocks, watch for falling debris from above. Sometimes you can find rocks polished by the water-and-sand action that reveal some really nice specimens. Again, as you search layers of rock sediment begin vertically until you find fossils and then move horizontally. Because of the wave action, look along the lakeshore to find more fossils. Also in the spring, just after the ice melts, new fossils are washed up on the rocky beaches.

Lakeshore south of Petoskey. With the low water level
fossils can be found at the waters edge.
Corals and brachiopods can be found here.

Quarries – Quarries sometimes can yield the best fossils; however you must obtain permission from working quarries before entering. Usually limestone is the main rock sought during quarry operations. In some quarries other sedimentary rock is discarded in spoils piles. Shale is one of those types of rock. Spoils piles can be found around quarry sites, and in some cases quarry operators make these piles available to the public to hunt for fossils. The limestone itself sometimes yields nice fossils. However, the main disadvantage of limestone is that it is very hard and dense. Fossils preserved in limestone can be very difficult to expose and prepare. Should a really spectacular fossil be found, there are professional preparers that can manage the preparation of that fossil.

Again remember to contact the quarry operations office prior to arrival to obtain permission to get into the quarry. Personnel and phone numbers change over time so call information for each individual quarry and ask for the operations office. Plan to spend an entire day – especially if you go to an abandoned quarry. Once you get in, you won't want to come out. Here are a few to get you started:

Main Quarry Operations Office of
LaFarge North America in Alpena, Michigan

Main Quarry Operations Office of
Michigan Limestone Quarry,
Rogers City, Michigan

Main Quarry Operations Office of
St. Mary's Limestone Quarry,
Charlevoix, Michigan

Northeastern Michigan

Rockport Quarry, north of Alpena, Michigan

At this point it is highly recommended that a quality map or Michigan gazetteer be purchased to assist in finding quarries and roads and possible rock outcroppings.

There are many wonderful areas in Northeastern Michigan. You can find fossils nearly any place along the lakeshore or route 23 where you see rock exposures. By far the most prevalent fossils found are those of various species of corals. Also, the area is checkered with limestone quarries. Some of the quarries are still in use and some are now closed. Please by all means, contact the management of the working quarries BEFORE you enter.

The rock formations on the northeastern side of the state have names such as *Rockport Quarry Limestone, Bell Shale, Norway Point Formation, Four Mile Dam Formation, Potter Farm Formation, Newton Creek Formation, Alpena Limestone, Thunder Bay Limestone, Squaw Bay Limestone, Genshaw Formation, Rogers City Limestone, Ferron Point Formation* and others. The names correspond to major names or locations where the outcroppings are found. They also give you an idea of where to look.

• Beginning just south of Alpena city limits on US 23 is Partridge Point. This is a location that is surrounded by private property. There is a private marina and many private residences. The north side of the point is the best location. Along the north shore you will see shale and rock just above the waterline. This is the best collecting along the point. At the western end of the point is a dirt road two track. This road leads out to state land along the lakeshore. Any collecting other than that along the state land lakeshore must be done after gaining the property owner's permission. There are many other places in the Alpena area that are accessible by public access.

Partridge Point Road, north

- Paxton Quarry just west of Alpena along route 32 is currently an inactive quarry. The quarry is owned and operated by Lafarge Corporation. The quarry has corals, shells and other flora and fauna. You must first obtain permission from Lafarge North America Corporation in Alpena. Along the eastern edge of the quarry you will find areas full of paper shale, shale that is very brittle and small. Very little is found in the way of fossils in that shale. The limestone in the area is the best rock in which to look. Corals and brachiopods can be found in this quarry. Since the quarry operations have ceased, it is beginning to fill with water. **Stay out of the water as the depths are varied and can drop off suddenly.**

Paxton Quarry, west of Alpena, Michigan

- The Lafarge North America, Alpena Cement Plant main quarry is located right in Alpena. As of this writing, the management of the Lafarge Quarry realized the importance of the rich paleonto logical heritage this site represents. The management does allow collectors into the quarry occasionally, but appointments must be made far ahead of time. You must contact the main quarry office and make an appointment to come to the quarry. Quarry officials will escort you on a tour and you will be allowed to collect in certain areas. You will be required to read and sign a release form. Also, you will be required to wear a hard hat, eye protection and steel toe protection. If you have any of the protective equipment, it is a good idea to bring it along.

Some great fossils have been removed from this quarry including some spectacular trilobites. There are several areas where quarry operators have deposited huge limestone blocks that are layered with thousands of shells. These shells are weathering out of the rock at a fantastic rate. Tools are not even required. Crinoid stems, bryozoans and several types of corals can also be found, but the sheer volume of brachiopods is staggering. You will be able to fill a bucket in the matter of 15 to 20 minutes. The guide assigned to take you into the quarry will gladly describe the formations and show you some spectacular fossil locations.

Many of the dirt access roads just north of the quarry also have dirt piles near the side of the roadways. The majority of fossils found in this area are coral and bryozoans. Brachiopods are also common but not as common as the corals. In some areas limestone blocks are placed across some access roads. Stop and check them out as they also contain many fossils.

The photograph below shows what is commonly called a bioherm. A bioherm is a rock formation that was once a coral reef. The bioherm looks like a mound or is somewhat lens-shaped. These ancient reef structures are comprised of the calcium carbonate skeletons and shells of many reef dwelling brachiopods and corals. In the photo below, the area within the rectangle is a Devonian bioherm. Just left of center the slope of the bioherm is clearly seen. The lighter colored material is the remains of the ancient reef.

Lafarge Quarry west wall showing a bioherm

- At the Alpena public marina and boat launch there are some large limestone blocks along the breakwater. There is no collecting here but you can see some coral and shell fossils in the large limestone blocks. It will give a novice collector an idea of what the fossils look like.

- North of Lafarge Quarry are many dirt access roads and dirt county roads. Along these roads there are occasionally embankments made of dirt and stone usually in the form of spoils piles from the quarry. In these embankments one can also find rock containing fossils.

- Traveling north from Alpena you come across Rockport Quarry, an abandoned quarry that now contains a state park and boat launch. As you travel north along US 23, you will drive along Long Lake until you come upon Rockport Road. There is also a sign for Rockport Harbor Public Access. Follow the road for 3 miles until you reach the park area. Park in the parking area and then go inland from the lakeshore. There are several dirt access roads; however, they are blocked by dirt piles. Keep heading west until you reach the abandoned quarry.

This quarry is quite large and has a great wealth of fossils. As is shown in the photos below, there are spoils piles just dumped all around the quarry in rows. There are numerous coral, bryozoan and brachiopod species in them. Parking is available at the old quarry and you'd better have good hiking shoes as you'll have to walk to get to the best areas. The fossils are located in the quarry to the west of the lakeshore and parking lot. There is a large lime stone pile visible, but the best hunting is done in the old quarry bed and spoils piles.

Spoils piles at Rockport Quarry. These piles contain numerous fossils including some brachiopod and many species of corals.

- Burkholder Road site and Sytek Park. This is one of the most fossiliferous sites in the state. It is also one of my personal favorites. This location has literally millions of fossils just lying on the ground ready to be picked up. The location demands a great deal of respect for nature and proper dig etiquette. This site must be preserved for future generations and fossil collecting.

  Traveling west on route 32, turn right on Bagley Road. The first intersection is a dirt road, Burkholder Road. The parking is best if you turn right into a small turnoff on the opposite side called Sytek Park. There is a gazebo and picnic tables and ample parking. If you have crossed the river, you have gone too far.

  The area doesn't look like much but wait until you see the fossils. **NO TOOLS** are needed; please don't dig, it is not necessary. As you go down into the roadside ditch, on the north side of the road, just look down. The best thing to do is to get down on your knees and start looking. Mother Nature is your best friend here. The sediment is so soft that rainwater washes the sediments away leaving the fossils behind just laying on the ground. You will see brachiopods, corals, crinoid stems, on and on. Make sure you bring a small bucket to put your finds in. Actually all of the ditches in that area and on the side where Sytek Park is also have fossils. Between Sytek Park and the section of retail stores there is a field of grass and scrub trees. Here one can also find many corals, bryozoans, brachiopods and other fossils.

View of Burkholder Road (to the south) from
Bagley Road, Alpena, Michigan

- As you cross the bridge on Bagley Road, west of Alpena, just north of the Thunder Bay River, you will see Long Rapids Road. Several miles after turning west on Long Rapids Road are 4 Mile and 7 Mile dams. Each of these dams has a formation named after it and these areas also have fossil exposures. The exposures are close to the water line so be careful when looking in these locations.

- As you travel west along route 32, just about 2 miles from Bagley Road is Lake Winyah Road. Turning right (north) on Lake Winyah Road you will come to a bend in the road. Straight ahead is property owned by Alpena Power Company. It is private; however, along the side of the road is a dirt and rock berm. In this berm can be found many corals and brachiopods.

- Traveling north on US 23 just outside of Alpena, turn left onto French Road. The road has a few twists and turns but follow it north to LaComb Road. Turn right and there will be a small abandoned quarry on the left. It is now privately owned. Ask permission at the house in front of the quarry. There are numerous examples of corals and shells. I found an excellent trilobite tail section within the first 2 minutes.

- Traveling north on US 23, travel toward Presque Isle. Turn right on Grand Lake Road. After several miles you will see the LaFarge Quarry sign. Turn onto the property. There will be many signs warning visitors to report to the office. Please travel down the access road until you reach the main office. Again, by the time you arrive, you should have made contact with the quarry operations office and have an appointment to go in and hunt fossils.

View into the LaFarge North America, Presque Isle Quarry

- Traveling north on US 23 toward Rogers City, several roadside exposures of rocks can be seen. Pull your vehicle well to the side of the road and turn on the hazard lights. Please, above all remain safe when collecting. These roadcuts into Rogers City can be productive. Mostly colony corals and bryozoans are found here. Beware of glacial till and lakeshore deposition. In some areas you will see large areas of rounded rocks. These rocks are the remains of glacial till and the weathering of rock by water action. In most cases this rock is not fossiliferous.

- Just before coming into Rogers City, turn right onto Business 23 toward the city. There s a scenic turnout on

Quarry View Road. At the end of the road you will see the entire quarry before you. It is a nice view of the entire quarry. Continue to the Michigan Limestone Calcite Quarry in Rogers City. Again, you must contact quarry operations and they will be glad to make an appointment for you.

**Panoramic view of Michigan Limestone Quarry
in Rogers City**

Northwestern Michigan

There are several rock outcroppings that are fossiliferous on the western side of Michigan. Running inland from the lakeshore, there are numerous locations where fossils may also be found. The formations bearing fossils have familiar names, such as the *Petoskey Formation, Whiskey Creek Formation, Gravel Point Formation, Norwood Shale, Ellsworth Shale, Antrim Shale* and so on. As you can see, the formations are named after towns, districts, townships and other areas. Looking in roadcuts, quarries both active and abandoned, as well as other locations will reward the rockhounds with some nice fossils.

Beginning at the Mackinaw Bridge, south on the western side of the state, following route 31 south from just north of Petoskey to Charlevoix is very fossil rich. Many exposures can be found along public access areas near the lakeshore. The limestone bluffs can be very high. When collecting in these areas, special attention must be paid to falling rock. IT IS HIGHLY RECOMMENDED that you wear a hard hat and steel-toed shoes.

Falling rock is a common occurrence near these cliffs, especially in the spring after the heavy spring rains. Ironically enough, it is in these new fall areas where some of the best fossils can be found.

Petoskey is well known for many exposures of fossils. The world famous and Michigan state stone "Petoskey Stone" is named after the Petoskey formation.

Beginning in the city of Petoskey, downtown marina district, one can follow Bayfront Drive. The drive ends in a turn around just below Sunset Park. Along the right side of Bayfront Drive you will see a cliff wall. Along the roadway the cliff rises from the road elevation.

Here is a long view of the cliffs at Sunset Park in Petoskey

Within rocks of this cliff is a very large stromatoporid reef. The stromatoporids are easily seen. They can be spotted in profile as in the oval on the right in the photo below shows, and you can actually see the stromatoporids in the oval on the left.

Layers of the stromatoporids can be seen on the right and the fossil coral itself on the left. Notice the "bumpy" texture of the stromatoporids on the left.

You can easily see the layers of the stromatoporid. A new generation grows on top of the old creating a striated colony as seen from the side. This location is extremely rich. Do not collect the corals off the rock face. This is a city park area and collecting off the cliff is not allowed. However, along the base of the cliff there is a great deal of rock that has tumbled off the cliff face. Here you can find exceptional stromatoporid specimens. The lakeshore along Little Traverse Bay is dotted with areas of rock outcroppings. Much of this land is now privately owned property. Along the lakeshore are many cliffs, and again much of the land is in private or state hands. Before collecting anywhere along the shores of Little Traverse Bay, please check with the owners prior to collecting any fossils.

Just south of Charlevoix along the lakeshore near the St. Mary's Cement Company Plant next to the Fisherman's Island State Park, just at the water's edge and going out into the bay is another location that bears describing. Turning west onto Bells Bay Road, follow the road down toward the quarry gate. Just before the gate the road turns left. Follow the road down to the dead end at the lakeshore. To the left is Fisherman's Island State Park. To the right is a dirt access road. Along this road are little turn offs where you can park your car and take the path to the water's edge. As you approach the dead end of the dirt road, your way will be blocked by three large rocks. One large rock approximately 6 feet tall and 6 feet wide is made up of hexegonaria and other corals. The smallest rock in the middle is almost completely covered by corals.

Follow the little dirt path to the water's edge and look down. Bring a sturdy hammer and chisel, you will need it. You are walking on bedrock millions of years old and you will see corals and shells that lived in the ancient

One of the paths to the water's edge from the dirt access road

Lakeshore view south toward Fisherman's Island

Devonian seas.

Lakeshore view north toward the concrete plant

This lakeshore is fossil rich. Make sure you bring a hammer and chisel. The bedrock you are walking on is the floor of the ancient salt water sea. You will see remains of the animals that lived here millions of years ago.

Southern Michigan/Ohio Border

Quarries of southern Michigan have yielded some very nice fossils. The deposits extend into northern Ohio, and in one location near Sylvania, Ohio, the exposures are close to the surface and are being quarried. On the western side of Sylvania at Olander Park. It is operated by the City of Sylvania. The quarry is along Centennial Road. From US 23 South, take the first Ohio exit just over the state line. Follow the exit to Monroe St. Turn left onto Monroe and follow it to the intersection of Erie. Actually, Monroe turns into Erie. Continue on Erie to Centennial and turn left on Centennial. The signs for fossil park are about 1/8 mile on the right, across from Mayberry Square. The fossil park is very fossil rich. The quarry operators bring loads of fossil laden sediment to the park and deposit it in piles so that the public can dig through it. No tools are allowed in the area except a brush and a bucket. There are no hammers allowed, however you will not need them. The sediment is quite loose and the fossils can be found just by digging through the sediment. The city has changed the operational hours from time to time, so it is best to call ahead to see if the fossil park is open.

The City of Sylvania has created a nice collecting area with covered tables, water for washing the fossils and other amenities to make the collecting experience more fun.

View of the signage at Olander Fossil Park

Overview of Fossil Park   View of collecting area

The area just over the boarder into Ohio, and all the way to Dundee there are numerous quarries, some abandoned and some working. One such quarry is just off exit 1 on US 23. This road is Sterns Road. Upon exiting

23 take Sterns Rd. to the east for a few miles. The working quarries rarely let collectors into the quarries except for special programs for school children and college classes. Sometimes rock clubs are also allowed to come and collect. These instances are rare. The current insurance regulations are too restrictive in many cases. Again in working quarries, it is best to call ahead and get permission to come in and dig through the spoils piles. Several of the quarries are operated by STONECO Construction Materials.

The area of southern Michigan has yielded some excellent examples of Pleistocene animals. Many examples of mastodons, several examples of mammoths as well as many other mammals have been found preserved in the sediments of southern Michigan. Most of these fossils, however, are usually found by accident by farmers and construction workers.

Picture Guide to Michigan Fossils

Fossils of the Paleozoic

The Paleozoic saw rise to what has been called the Cambrian explosion and it saw the extinction of nearly 90% of life on earth at the end of the Permian Period. Organisms began very primitively and evolved to bigger and better creatures. Most of the life on earth was concentrated in the oceans of the world for approximately 175 million years. It wasn't until the Silurian Period (430 – 395 million years ago) that primitive plants began to colonize the earth.

CORALS

Corals are simple aquatic animals that are credited with the formation of reefs and in some cases islands in the ocean. Corals are important rock builders because they are comprised of calcium carbonate exoskeletons that are essential in the formation of limestone. Corals are usually the most common fossil found in Paleozoic fossil deposits. Two common types of coral found here are solitary and colony corals. Their names suggest the way they evolved. Solitary corals such as horn coral grow by themselves and colony corals grow in tight groups.

Solitary Corals

Solitary corals, also sometimes called horn corals, can grow to be very large. Solitary corals are just that, they live ostensibly by themselves. The corals attach to rocks or other hard surfaces singly. Although they are solitary, sometimes they can live clustered together; however, they are not attached together along the length of the coral.

Colony Corals

Colony corals are just that. Individual creatures that live together in a group. The corals include corals like the cylindrophyllum, growing on tall columns side by side to the hexagonaria, the well-known coral that rock shops make into the Petoskey stone, the state fossil of Michigan.

Colony corals are mutually supportive and can be considered as reef builders. They also grow in large colonies providing cover and concealment for other creatures.

Normal reef development, the ebb and flow of sand back and forth provide a base for entire habitats for organisms.

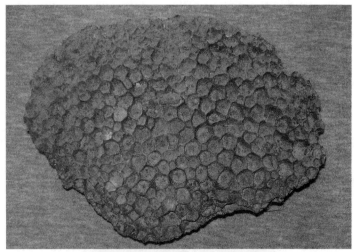

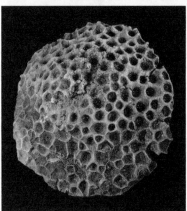

Hexagonaria coral head

Stromatopora

This is a type of coral that grows in very large colonies. These are also considered reef builders as you can find huge areas containing these corals making up entire cliff faces. As you can see in the photo, they grow in sheets. A cross section of the coral can be easily seen. The top of the coral is covered by little bumps.

Top: Stromatopora at Sunset Park, Petoskey, Michigan
Bottom: Stromatopora from the Lafarge Quarry, Alpena, Michigan

Rugose corals

Rugose corals are also commonly called horn corals or cup corals. They can be solitary, that is living singly or colonial, living in large associated groups. They have a hard solid exoskeleton. This exoskeleton is the part that usually fossilizes. Most horn corals have septa that radiate from the center to the outer edge. The septa are the divisions in the corallite that radiate from the center of the corallite. Horn corals are generally cone shaped with the point of origin usually the base or bottom of the coral on the wide part with the opening being the top. Colonial corals can be very long and tubular using each other for support. There are also very short and wide colonial corals.

Tabulate corals

Tabulate corals are colonial corals. Examples of these corals exhibit long, thin and straight corallites or tubes. They do not exhibit prominent septa. Tabulate corals are extinct. They lived only during the Paleozoic Period and did not survive past the Permian Period.

Bethanyphyllum

This solitary coral is very robust. This coral is considered a horn coral for obvious reasons. The coral begins attached to the sea floor at a point and then grows upward and outward. It is very cone or "horn" shaped. The top of the coral has a cone shaped depression. The septa are very distinct and normally visible in weathered or prepared specimens. The coral is often found 3-6 inches long. Smaller specimens are found and are normally well preserved.

Bethanyphyllum coral

Cystiphylloides

This coral is usually found as a solitary coral. These types are found in abundance in the northern Lower Peninsula. The coral is cylindrical in shape sometimes being slightly cone-shaped. The exterior of the coral looks slightly wrinkled. The corals can be up to 10 inches long and can be as large as several inches wide. They are usually found in lengths from 1 to 3 inches long. Longer sections are very desirable.

Cystiphylloides coral

Cylindrophyllum

This coral grows in large colonies, and can be readily identified by its shape. The *Cylindrophyllum* coral has very round corallites and tops of the coral. They normally grow tall and are generally the same diameter from bottom to top. The *Cylindrophyllum* corals are commonly found in many areas of the state and are a major reef builder of the ancient Paleozoic seas.

Cylindrophyllum coral

Prismatophyllum and Hexagonaria

This coral is a colonial coral. It is one of the most famous corals in the State of Michigan. The coral grows in large coral heads. Some have been found several feet across. Each individual corallite usually has 5 or 6 sides. There is a small depression in the center of each corallite as well. Many rock shops sell this coral sliced and polished. It is known as the famous Petoskey stone, the Michigan state fossil. When polished the corals show the great detail of each individual corallite with its septa. *Hexagonaria* is found in the upper Midwest and Michigan. *Prismatophyllum* is very common and found throughout fossil bearing strata in Michigan.

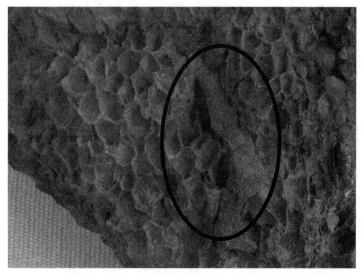

Example of a *Prismatophyllum* coral with a *Favosites alpenensis* piece lying across the center

Favosites

There are many species of this tabulate coral. All have a diminutive individual corallite within the colony coral. Some of the coral heads are massive. Cross sections can be seen in many broken pieces of limestone. It can be found throughout the state. The individual corallites are small and loosely packed. They are also sometimes called honeycomb corals. These corals can be quite small but are normally found in much larger chunks.

The photo below is of a *Favosites* that is quite unusual. This one is beautifully formed as it formed on a rock over 300 million years ago. The rock it formed on has since separated leaving a great looking coral head. There are also remnants of crinoids and brachiopods that fell on top of the coral head prior to fossilization.

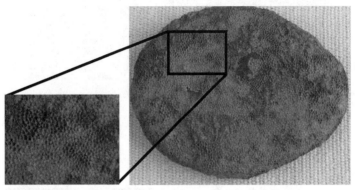

Nearly perfect example of a *Favosites* colony that was formed on a rock. Each "dimple" or hole contained a tiny creature.

Favosites memmillatus

This *Favosites* coral species is sheet-like with prominent bumps that rise from the sheet-like surface. The corals can be massive, covering large areas. These corals are also reef builders and can be found in very large colonies. The walls between the corallites are very thin but definitely visible.

Favosites memmillatus

Favosites alpenensis

This species of *Favosites* looks like broken branches of a tree. Most of the time these fossils are found in the condition shown in the photograph. Entire colonies are seldom well preserved. Each individual holes or indentations on the surface of this bryozoan contained one creature.

Favosites alpensis

Aulocystis fenestrate

Aulocystis fenestrate

This tabulate coral is quite diminutive when found in certain strata. It can be found in large blocks of limestone but still is quite small. This coral grows like the branches of a tree. At the end of each branch is a hole where the creature would have lived.

Trachypora

This coral is very easy to identify. Normally only parts of this coral are found fossilized. The thick stems of this coral have numerous round holes in them. It is a branching coral and unfortunately is rarely found intact.

During the deposition, sedimentation and fossilization process, these fossils normally break into pieces and are what is found as fossils.

Trachypora

ECHINODERMS

This group of animals includes starfish, sea urchins, crinoids, blastoids and brittle stars. Echinoderms were normally solitary creatures. Even the crinoid, an animal that lived attached to rocks, had the ability to locomote or move somewhat around the ocean floor. All echinoderms have a hard calcite exoskeleton. Echinoderms also have "tube feet" that they use to attach themselves, in feeding, sensing the environment, respiration and in movement. There are 15 classes of extinct echinoderms. Several classes including the crinoids are still alive in the oceans today and have changed little in millions of years. As fossils go in the State of Michigan, there are over 40 different species of crinoids alone.

Crinoids

Sometimes called lilies of the sea and feather stars, crinoids are actually animals, not plants. These creatures were very abundant in the oceans. The crinoid's calcite skeleton was critical in the formation of many bedrock limestones. The central column or stem is made up of small disk-shaped segments that are stacked like poker chips. Once the creature dies, the structure falls apart leaving hundreds of such disks scattered on the ocean floor.

Crinoid stems and pieces in limestone

Loose crinoid stems and disks

The top crown, or calyx is made up normally of branched arms. These feather-like appendages filter the seawater in order to feed. The arms catch floating debris and move it down to the mouth. Crinoids were common throughout history and they are also found in the deep ocean today. What are normally found in many of the fossil deposits in Michigan are the disassociated stem pieces, calyx pieces, crinoid spikes and calyx plates. There are many species of crinoids found across Michigan.

Example of a crinoid stem, calyx
and "feathered" arms

Example of a
crinoid calyx
with arms

Various spikes from the
Gennaeocrinus goldringae

Various calyx pieces from the
Megistocrinus nodosus

Dolatocrinus calyx

Blastoids

Blastoids are small echinoderms that also have a small stem. The blastoids are similar in structure to the crinoids except that the theca or calyx is roughly rounded with normally 5 distinct petal-shaped divisions. There are small thread-like arms that projected upward from the theca. These were used for feeding. They fed on the floating material and plankton in the ancient seas.

Blastoids are found less frequently in the sediments than crinoids. They seemed to have lived in small colonies in association with other crinoids and corals. In several areas of Michigan they can be found in close proximity to each other and absent in many other areas of the state.

Heteroschisma latum

Heteroschisma

This small blastoid has been found in the Potter Farm Formation of Alpena. These creatures grew on a small stem just like crinoids. The blastoid is roughly cone-shaped and slender from bottom to top. There is a 5 pointed star shaped top with 5 radiating "petals." This species is considered more primitive than other blastoids. They are quite rare until you find an area where a colony was.

Tentaculites

Tetaculites undescribed

These creatures are still a bit of a mystery to paleontologists. They defy current classification. They are very small creatures similar in size to a pencil lead. The fossil comes to a point and radiates up from there. They are normally found clustered together in matrix of the sea floor. In certain sediments around Alpena they can be found completely free of matrix in the sediment. A sifting screen must be used in order to find them. It is not known if they were free swimming or lived attached to the bottom of the sea.

BRYOZOANS

These creatures are sometimes called "moss animals." They are a minute colonial creature that either forms branching, encrusting or sheet-like growths. The encrusting bryozoans grow on rocks as well as other underwater structures like dead corals. Branching bryozoans resemble corals. Each individual indentation or hole in the bryozoan contained a tiny creature that resembled the modern sea anemone. The creature had tiny tentacles and was a filter feeder.

Fenestella

Fenestella

This creature lived in large colonies that appeared lattice-like in structure. Similar to the sea fans of today, these creatures grew attached to rocks, shells and other underwater structures. Typically these creatures are found broken and in small pieces. They were a filter feeder; the lattice-like structure allowing the water to flow freely through it.

BRACHIOPODS

These ancient creatures abounded in the seas of the Paleozoic Era. Sometimes called lamp shells, these once-common invertebrates are some of the most easily recognized fossils. Of the nearly 30,000 species of brachiopods that were once common in the seas, only about 200 species survive today. These primitive seashells came in many forms. Usually they comprise two unequal halves also called valves. These halves are attached at a hinge line. There is normally a hole in the center of the hinge through which the stalk passes. The shells are made up of calcium phosphate and chitin. The shells were held together by internal muscles. Some brachiopods grew to 9 inches long, but most were only about an inch in diameter. They did not move around a great deal on the ocean floor. They spent most of their time attached to the ocean floor by a long fleshy stalk. In certain areas around the state, one may actually find shell halves. As the brachiopods died, they sometimes split in half along the hinge line. These halves would then fossilize. In the Alpena area the sediment has allowed these delicate fossils to become exposed. I have found numerous brachiopods on the "halfshell." These fossils expose the internal structure of the shell. The muscle attachment areas and hinge line can be easily seen.

Mucrospirifer

Example of *Mucrospirifer* brachiopods
found in Alpena, Michigan

This shell is quite impressive when found complete.
Unfortunately, most of these shells are found with the
"wings" broken off. The shell is very wide, up to 4 inches
long in some species. The shell is widest at the hinge line.
Both valves are convex. The center of the shell has a very
deep furrow that goes from the top to the hinge line. The
ventral valve is slightly convex and the dorsal valve is very
convex.

Strophodonta

Strophodonta

This shell is quite common in some deposit. The shell is approximately 1 inch long. It is roughly semicircular in shape. The shell of the complete creature is quite thin. The ventral or bottom side is convex and the dorsal or top side is concave. The exterior of the shell is covered in very fine radiating ribs. The shell is at its widest along the hinge line. Sometimes these shells can be found as halves only. If the preservation is good, one can see the areas of muscle attachment and small ridges along the hinge line.

Cyrtina

A small shell usually 1/4 inch long. Looking at the ventral side, the shell is very triangular in shape. The base is also very flat. The dorsal side has very broad ribs. It is believed that this brachiopod stayed flat on the sea bed. Many species of cyrtina can be found in one area. In some species the central point of the hinge can be slightly curved.

Athyris

Athyris

This brachiopod grew to approximately 1 to 2 inches long. The shell was usually rounded to roughly oval in shape. The hinge line is rather short in this species. Both valves, halves of the shell, are convex with the ventral being slightly convex and the dorsal being convex. The dorsal and ventral sides are roughly the same thickness. Concentric growth lines can be seen on the exterior of the shell. There is a small round opening at the hinge where the stalk would come out of in order to attach to the sea floor.

Many fossils of this species can be found with a second hole somewhere on the dorsal valve of the shell. This is evidence of gastropod predation. The gastropods would use their rasping jaws to drill a hole in the shell and then eat the creature inside.

Atrypa

Atrypa

This is a very plentiful brachiopod in the sediments in which they are found. They are some of the most common brachiopods in the fossil record. The shell is usually less than 1 inch in diameter but larger specimens have often been found. This brachiopod has a very large and bulbous top valve. The bottom valve is much smaller and flatter. In some deposits the shell is so common that it is nearly the only fossil found. In some cases both the *Athyris* and *Atrypa* can be found with a hole in the dorsal valves near the top of the shells. This is due to predation by other creatures such as gastropods or mollusks.

Pentamerella

Pentamerella alpenensis

There are several species of *Pentamerella*. Most notably *alpenensis* and *petoskeyensis* species. They can grow to approximately 1 inch in diameter. They are easily identified by the large ribbed shell. They are not as frequent as the *Atrypa, Athyris, Mucrospirifer* and *Strophodonta* shells.

GASTROPODS

The class gastropoda includes the snails. Most gastropods have a single, usually spirally coiled shell into which the body can be withdrawn. Fossil gastropods had a muscular foot which was used for locomotion in most of the species. In some, it is modified for swimming or burrowing. Most gastropods had a well-developed head that included eyes, 1 to 2 pairs of tentacles, and a concentration of nervous tissue (ganglion). The mouth consisted of a jaw filled with rasping teeth. Some evidence exists that the gastropods would feed on the shelled brachiopods. Fossils of brachiopods can be found with small drilled holes which give us evidence of the rasping teeth gastropods used in feeding.

Pleurotomaria alpenensis

Pleurotomaria alpenensis

This gastropod can be found in the Devonian strata around Alpena. Specifically found in some abundance in the Potter Farm Formation. Usually the fossil is not well preserved as the original permineralized shell is quite thin. Most fossils are found as molds and casts, some-times with the brittle external shell preserved.

Omphalocirrus

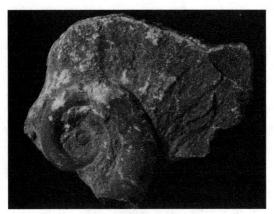

Omphalocirrus

Found in the Rogers City Formation of Rockport Quarry, this fossil has a tightly coiled shell that begins very small and ends up very large near the opening. Although many confuse this creature with cephalopods, it is really a gastropod. They are rarely found in the sediments and can grow to several inches across.

CEPHALOPODS

Cephalopods are an ancient group that appeared some time in the late Cambrian period several million years before the first primitive fish began swimming in the ocean. Cephala means head and pod means foot. Scientists believe that the ancestors of modern cephalopods–octopus, squid, and cuttlefish–diverged from the primitive externally shelled Nautilus very early, perhaps in the Ordovician, some 438 million years ago. They normally have a long bullet shape, but some species still have a rounded shell. The internal structure of the long bullet-shaped belemnites was a hard cartilage that was the only part that fossilized. These can be found in Michigan. But most often one can find the external shells of both the elongated and circular cephalopods. These creatures were believed to be predators. Having tentacles, they were able to catch and grasp prey creatures. What is normally found as fossils are these hard external shells. The soft parts including tentacles have long since decayed.

Platyceras

This is an interesting creature. Many specimens have been found attached to crinoids. This seems to be a symbiotic relationship. The *Platyceras* are found attached to the anal tube, the waste evacuation tube of a crinoid. It seems that the *Platyceras* would feed on the discharge from the crinoids. As mass extinctions or localized extinction and rapid burial events happened, the crinoids and *Platyceras* would be buried just as they were in life. Hence we have proof that the *Platyceras* lived at least part of their lives in symbiosis with the crinoids.

PLANTS

Up to the Devonian period, land plants were rare. Only primitive land plants, like club mosses and primitive trees, lived on the earth. During the Devonian period the land plants began to develop more complex forms. Much of what is found as plant fossils in the state can be found as carbonized masses of the branches of these plants. Some large stumps and trunks of trees have been found in the state, and many have found their way to museums.

One of the most common fossil trees found in Michigan is the calymites. There are several areas around the state where Pennsylvanian rocks have been found. Most are in old coal mines and mine dump locations in the area around Midland and Saginaw. One can also find various types of plants and ferns in this coal bearing strata. The Saginaw Formation contains many of these fossils and can also be found in Grand Ledge.

TRILOBITES

Trilobites are an extinct form of arthropod. Today arthropods include insects, spiders, crabs, crayfish, lobsters and the closest living relative, the horseshoe crab. Trilobites lived in the shallow salt water seas that were once Michigan. The trilobites were alive from the Cambrian explosion of life until the end of the Permian period when 90 % of life on earth became extinct.

Trilobites have a hard exoskeleton broken up into 3 distinct lobes, hence the name Tri-Lobe-ite. It is divided vertically into one axial lobe that runs down the middle of the trilobite and 2 pleural lobes on either side. It is also divided horizontally into 3 sections–the head section or cephalon, the body section or thorax, and the tail section or pygidium. The thorax could be made up of as little as 2 segments or as many as 32 segments.

The trilobite was the first creature on earth with primitive eyes, similar to a fly's eye. It had antennae and one pair of walking legs and gill branches per each thoracic body segment. They were believed to be scavengers feeding on the decaying plant and animal matter on the bottom of the ocean and occasionally could catch and eat primitive bottom dwelling creatures. In order to grow the trilobite had to molt or shed the exoskeleton. The shed pieces are what is usually found as fossils. Once the exoskeleton is shed, it falls apart on the ocean floor.

Occasionally one can find a complete trilobite, truly an exceptional find.

Phacops

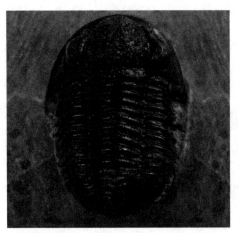

Example of a *Phacops* trilobite

This trilobite is most commonly found in southern Michigan and northern Ohio. It is a very common trilobite in the deposits in which it is found and also easily identifiable. The head section is semi-circular, and the trilobite itself is generally oval in shape. The head section is very bulbous and inflated with numerous tubercles. The head section also has two large crescent-shaped eyes that usually exhibit outstanding detail. One can easily see the many lenses of the eyes. The average size of this trilobite is 1-2 inches long. Several specimens can be found that are much larger. In the area of northern Ohio, near Sylvania, the trilobites are often found enrolled – rolled up in tiny balls, similar to the "rolly polly" or pill bug.

Greenops

The *Greenops* trilobite can be found in the area of northern Lower Peninsula as well as in Arkona, Ontario, Canada. The *Greenops* has a semicircular head section that ends in two medium length spines. The center or glabella of the head section is furrowed. It has two crescent-shaped eyes. The tail section and the thorax segments end in short spines. This trilobite can also be easily identified. In many cases all that is found of this trilobite is discarded pieces of the exoskeleton.

Deschenella

This trilobite is usually quite small, less than 1 inch to 1 inch long. The trilobite is fairly oval in shape. It has a semi circular head section that ends in two small spines. This trilobite has a large number of body segments. The tail section is roughly triangular in shape. The axial or middle lobe of the trilobite thorax is quite wide at the head section and tapers to a thin lobe by the time it ends at the tip of the tail section. Again, most of what is found as a fossil is disarticulated body sections.

Some other trilobites that can be found in the state are
Basidechenella
Crassiproetus
Dipleura

FISH

As far back as the Devonian period, primitive sharks and fish began to develop and flourish. However finding the fossilized remains of fish is difficult. In many cases fish and sharks are comprised of cartilage or cartilaginous bone and were not prone to fossilization. Usually the soft cartilage and bone material decayed long before fossilization could occur. There are however several primitive fish that had hard, boney plates covering the outside of their bodies, much like armor. These plates often did fossilize. In some cases, teeth and jaws from primitive fish and sharks also fossilized. Remains nonetheless are very rare and often found disarticulated and are often hard to identify. As the fish decay, scavengers, waves and water action tended to disarticulate the fish, spreading the remains around the sea floor. The area of northern Lower Peninsula between Alpena, Rockport and Onaway has produced some specimens of fossilized fish.

Fossils of the Pleistocene

Finding fossils from near the end of this epoch, just after the last Ice Age are usually purely accidental. Many of these fossils are found in farmers' fields as they plow for crops or by workers and contractors digging foundations or new roadcuts. In other cases, sand and gravel excavation also uncovers skeletal components. These fossils are quite important to research into the Ice Age of Michigan. Some bones have been found with post-mortem cutmarks on them, indicating some type of human activity was involved. The majority of the fossil evidence is of mastodons. Relatively few of the other types of mammals that once lived here have been found. And in many cases all that is found are the teeth of these creatures.

Since the finding of fossil vertebrate material is rather rare, it is important to either leave the fossils in situ (where they lie) or turn them over to museum or university authorities.

In some cases the universities and museums have cleaned the fossil, made a mold and cast of it and then returned the original fossil to the finder. But because vertebrate remains are so rare and scientifically important it is equally important to have them turned in and properly documented and prepared.

Jefferson mammoths
(Mammuthus jeffersoni) extinct

Mammoths are known in Michigan by the few remains found within the state. These larger cousins of the mastodons were grazers and inhabited areas of large open grassland spaces. Mammoths had large teeth that were flattened on top with ridges traversing the tooth from side to side. The mammoth would chew their food from side to side, much like a modern cow, grinding the food along the ridges of the tooth. Since the state was covered mostly by forests, and the area further north into Canada was more like tundra grassland, mammoth remains can be more readily found north of Michigan. Sixteen sites have been found around the State of Michigan.

American mastodons
(Mammut americanum) extinct

The mastodons were animals that resembled the modern elephants except that they had long fur. They were smaller than their cousins the mammoths. The mastodons lived in the woodland forests that once covered the state. Their main food was the branches of the forest trees. The teeth of a mastodon were designed to crunch and grind the branches they chose as food. The mastodon would chew in an up and down manner much the same as we do. Quite different than the side to side manner of the mammoth. Their remains can be found across the state usually in the remnants of ancient bogs. The southern part of the state from Ann Arbor to Grand Rapids seems to be the richest in mastodon remains. Often it seems that farmers tilling their fields are the discoverers of these long-since extinct creatures. Over 100 sites have been found in Michigan, nearly all in southern Michigan.

OTHER MAMMALS OF MICHIGAN

Numerous remains have been found and turned over to the University of Michigan Museum of Paleontology. Some examples of creatures can be found in local historical society museums as well. Many creatures found in Pleistocene deposits are creatures that still inhabit the woodlands of Michigan today. However some of these creatures are now extinct. Finding remains of these now-extinct creatures is quite rare. The fossilization process as we have learned takes time and the conditions must be perfect for the preservation of organic material. In many cases only teeth or skull fragments are found.

Giant beaver
(Castoroides ohioensis) extinct

The giant beaver grew to a length of approximately

7 feet long. There have only been 5 sites found where remains of the giant beaver have been recovered. Of these sites, only small pieces including teeth, lower jaws and skulls have been found.

Woodland musk ox
(Symbos cavifrons) extinct

This creature was believed to be very common during the Pleistocene much as musk ox are common in northern Canada and Alaska today. Seven sites have been recorded in the state and all specimens are in the collection of the University of Michigan.

Scott's moose *(Cervalces scotti)* extinct

Only one specimen of this creature has been found in Michigan. It is an antler and was found in Berrien County.

Pecaries *(Platygonus compressus)* extinct

Remains of this extinct pig-like creature were found in the State of Michigan in 1877. They were found in a peat bog in Ionia County.

Whales and Walruses, Seals and Sea Lions

Rarely have remains been found in the state, but they

have been found. Again only small pieces of skeletons have been found. Nearly all the specimens are in the collection of the University of Michigan, Museum of Paleontology.

Finally ....

The reality is that there are not enough paleontologists in this country to make all the fossil discoveries needed. During a period in time long ago the conditions were just right for the formation of fossils. These fossils are just beneath our feet now due to another fact of earth science. Curiosity and the desire to learn more has allowed the science of paleontology to grow and begin to explain our Michigan prehistoric history.

Amateurs are important to the science of paleontology, in fact, many of the fossil discoveries including dinosaur discoveries in other states are made by amateurs. Michigan has a rich fossil heritage. Take the time to explore it, take time to travel around the state looking for these ancient treasures.

What a great way to spend time with your family as well. Vacations to the northern end of the Lower Peninsula can become rewarding in quality time spent with your family and the lure of discovery.

"...in disclosing the past of the earth... the mind of man is cultivated and kept open...."

–Leonardo DaVinci

References

Dorr, John A. and Donald Eschman. *Geology of Michigan.* Ann Arbor: The University of Michigan Press, 1970.

Ehlers, G.M. and R.V. Kesling. *Devonian Strata of Alpena and Presque Isle Counties, Michigan.* Ann Arbor: Michigan Basin Geological Society, 1970.

Holman, J. Alan. *Ancient Life of the Great Lakes Basin: Precambrian to Pleistocene.* Ann Arbor: The University of Michigan Press, 1995.

Kesling, R.V., A.M. Johnson and H.O. Sorensen. *Devonian Strata of Afton-Onaway Area, Michigan.* Papers on Paleontology, no.17. Ann Arbor: Museum of Paleontology, 1976.

Kesling, R.V., R.T. Segall and H.O. Sorensen. *Devonian Strata of Emmet and Charlevoix Counties, Michigan.* Papers on Paleontology, no.7. Ann Arbor: Museum of Paleontology, 1974.

Thompson, Ida. *National Audubon Society Field Guide to North American Fossils.* New York: Knopf, 1982.

Photo Credits

Roger Chase, Photographic Reverie
www.photographicreverie.com